RING OF FIRE

by Sonia Martinson
illustrated by Dave Sullivan

Harcourt

Orlando   Boston   Dallas   Chicago   San Diego

Visit *The Learning Site!*

www.harcourtschool.com

How is cold, icy Alaska similar to hot, humid Guatemala? How are both places similar to Hawaii, Japan, and Russia? They are all places at the edge of the Pacific Ocean. All of them are places where volcanoes and earthquakes have shaped the land. This land that rings the Pacific Ocean is known as the Ring of Fire.

The Earth is made up of many layers. The outer layers of Earth are made of rock. Under the Earth's solid outer crust, however, is a layer of hot liquid called *magma*. When magma cools, it forms new rock.

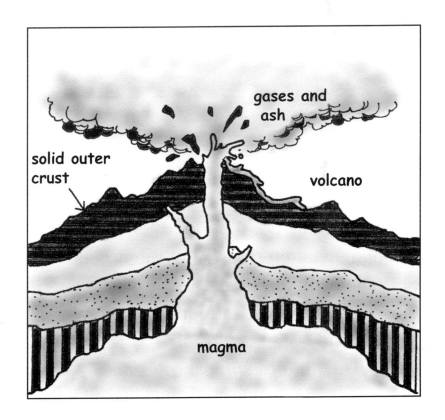

Volcanoes are openings in Earth's crust.
A volcano looks like a mountain, but it
often has a large opening at its peak.
Magma comes out through this opening or
through vents on the side of the mountain.
Sometimes it comes out slowly. At other
times, it comes out with great force. When
the magma comes out of the volcano,
people say that the volcano "erupts." When
volcanoes erupt, they send gases and ash
high into the air.

Lava—the magma that comes out of the volcano—flows over the land. It buries everything in its path. The lava can also pile up and form a cone-shaped mountain. The peak of this volcano may be thousands of feet high.

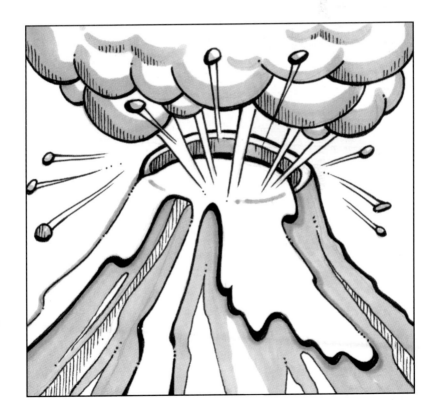

Volcanoes are either active or quiet. Active volcanoes show signs of erupting. Scientists study active volcanoes carefully, so that they can warn people who live near the volcanoes if they are going to erupt.

Quiet volcanoes have stopped erupting. Mt. Fuji in Japan is a quiet volcano. Many people from around the world visit Mt. Fuji. Many artists paint pictures of it.

Asia

North America

Ring of Fire

•Volcano

South America

Australia

Pacific Ocean

If you look at a map of the world's volcanoes, you'll find that most of them are around the edges of the Pacific Ocean. The Ring of Fire includes mountain ranges along the Pacific coast of North America and South America. It includes the east coast of Asia and the islands near the coast, such as Japan.

The islands in the Pacific Ocean are also part of the Ring of Fire. The Hawaiian Islands, for example, are really the peaks of an underwater mountain range. This range was formed by volcanoes on the ocean floor. The mountains are so tall that some of their peaks rise out of the water as islands. Much of this range is below the water, however.

Because volcanoes can erupt, you might think that people would never live near one. However, the ash that comes from a volcano makes some of the best soil on Earth. So a volcano's slopes may be very good land for farming. Two crops that grow well in this kind of soil are coffee beans and cacao beans.

Some volcanic mountain ranges are popular vacation spots. Some just happen to be where people live.

However, people must take care to stay safe. Because of this, scientists study volcanoes all over the world very carefully. Now they know what happens in an active volcano before it erupts.

Scientists also study earthquakes. An earthquake happens when Earth's crust suddenly shifts, or moves. (It is moving very, very slowly all the time.) The place where the earthquake starts is called the epicenter. The shaking of the Earth is strongest there.

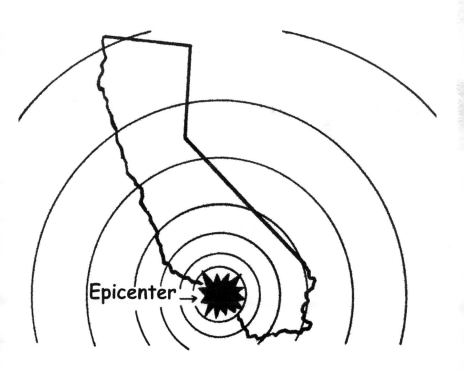

Epicenter

Strong earthquakes can do great damage to buildings, roads, and bridges. Many people can be hurt.

After a very strong earthquake, there are often smaller ones. These small earthquakes are called *aftershocks.*

A seismograph (SYZ•muh•graf) is one tool that scientists use to tell how strong an earthquake is. It tracks movement in Earth's crust. It uses a pen to make a record of this movement on paper. Seismographs are set up all over the world. They record between 40,000 and 50,000 earthquakes each year. However, only about 40 earthquakes do a lot of harm.

Some earthquakes are very strong. These quakes can be felt thousands of miles away. Strong earthquakes that occur on the bottom of the ocean can cause huge waves. These waves speed across thousands of miles. They have so much power that when they reach the coast they can wash away whole towns.

Scientists study volcanic eruptions and earthquakes so they can warn people before these disasters strike again. There is no way of knowing exactly when earthquakes will happen. However, scientists know where they are likely to happen. They also know how many years are likely to pass between earthquakes in an area.

Volcanoes, unlike earthquakes, give many warnings before they erupt. The ground may rise or sink. Certain gases come out of the ground, and small earthquakes are felt. Scientists use seismometers and other measuring tools to keep track of these changes. They know when to tell people, "It's time to go." These warnings have saved many lives.